What Your CPA Is NOT Telling You That Could Be Hurting Your Business

By Joseph D Rose, CPA, CTC

Desert Rose Tax & Accounting

5702 East 22nd Street

Tucson, AZ 85711

www.DesertRoseTax.com

Telephone: (520) 747-4964

Fax: (520) 747-4968

The information contained in this special report has been obtained from sources that are believed to be reliable. The publisher or author is not responsible for any errors, omissions, or damages, which may be caused by the use of information contained in this manual. It is sold/offered with the understanding that the publisher is not engaged in the rendering of legal, accounting, or other professional service. If legal advice or other expert assistance is required, the services of a competent professional person should be sought.

Copyright 2016

All rights reserved. The text of this publication, or any part thereof, may not be reproduced in any manner whatsoever without written permission from the publisher.

Published by:
Desert Rose Tax & Accounting, PC
Tucson, AZ, USA
www.DesertRoseTax.com

DEDICATION

This E-book is dedicated to my loving wife Sue. Without her unwavering support, this project could not have occurred.

TABLE OF CONTENTS

PART 1: Tax Reduction

Strategy #1: HSA Plan..11

Strategy #2: Home Office Write-off........................12

Strategy #3: College Education Write-off...............13

Strategy #4: Roth IRA Eligibility for Kids.................15

Strategy #5: Business Retirement Plans..................16

Strategy #6: Vehicle Deduction................................17

Strategy #7: Roth Conversions..................................18

PART II: Profit Maximization

Strategy #8: Pricing and Fees....................................21

Strategy #9: Accounting Firm Compatibility..........22

Strategy #10: Effective Accounting System............23

Strategy #11: Financial Responsibility....................24

Strategy #12: Gross vs. Net.......................................25

Strategy #13: Tracking Critical Numbers................26

Strategy #14: Cash vs. Profit.....................................27

Strategy #15: Customer's Lifetime Value............................27

Strategy #16: The Trap of ONE 29

Strategy #17: Customer Referrals..30

Strategy #18: Meaningful Touches...30

Strategy #19: Customer-centric Services.............................31

Strategy #20: Effective Communication...............................32

Strategy #21: Pay Yourself First...33

Strategy #22: Systemize to Reduce Stress...........................34

PART III: Asset Protection

Strategy #23: Protective Legal Structure.............................37

Strategy #24: Diversified Protection.....................................37

Strategy #25: Audit Protection...39

Next Steps

Financial Freedom is Only One Step Away.........................41

Your Roadmap To Success..44

Reserve My Spot...46

AN OPEN LETTER FROM Joseph D Rose, CPA, CTC

Dear Business Owner,

For nearly 20 years, I've been helping business owners like you "beat the tax man" using 100 percent legal tax-reduction and profit maximization strategies most CPA's have no clue about. That's why I'd like to share with you some secret strategies I've discovered and developed that will help you drastically minimize your tax bill.

With the help of my special report and the strategies within, I'm confident that you'll **put more money back into your pocket this year and (legally) beat the IRS at its own game**. The fact is, there's nothing in your business that hemorrhages cash flow like income taxes. For most business owners, it's the **largest** expense on their financial statement, yet most business owners take the hit without thinking of their options to, legally, get a large portion of it back into their bottom line.

Think about all the costs you control in maintaining your business: payroll, supplies, and lab fees. When it comes to income taxes, though, you most likely leave that in the hands of someone else. With this in mind, my question to you is: **Are you getting what you need from your CPA?**

In light of new tax changes, it's important you consider this question carefully. If you currently make up to $300,000 in your business per year, you're taxed at 28 percent federally. You've got Social Security and Medicare taxes at 15.2 percent. The state you live in takes another substantial bite of your income. Add all these together and almost half your income stream is going out the door due to income taxes.

You need a CPA who understands your business and can help you regain the money you're currently losing.

Your accountant should be one of the most valuable resources on your business's team— someone who is a strategic partner, who is an **expert** in tax minimization and profit maximization strategies—and not someone who merely handles your monthly accounting and prepares your year-end income tax return, because you shouldn't have to be just another client.

I understand the complex tax laws and intricacies of your business. Beyond that, I approach my work in the spirit of partnership. I'm here as a financial ally and coach to help you keep more of what you earn, day by day. My role is not to just fill out forms and tell you what you owe come Tax Day, but to work with you all year long.

I invite you to read this special report as an opportunity to simply get to know me better, learn my strategies and approach, and see what I can do for you. If you like what you read, I welcome you to join me for a free one-on-one strategy session so we can explore your particular situation in more detail. Working with my team and I is truly like getting the five-star service you deserve, all year long, without sacrificing more than is necessary to pay for it. Once you experience it yourself, you too will understand why so many professionals in Arizona choose Desert Rose Tax & Accounting.

Sincerely,

Joseph D Rose, CPA

Part 1: Tax Reduction

As the single largest expense people encounter in life—more than the cost of a home or sending kids to college—income taxes are the most prevalent barrier to real financial security. You can never build any real wealth without first getting your tax life under control. One third of wealth you will or won't accumulate is dependent on whether you have a good tax plan. You may have heard the expression "tax freedom day." That's the day when we stop working for the government and begin working for ourselves.

As an individual and business owner, your objective should always be to pay the least amount of taxes legally. My experience working with business owners indicates that they are paying much more in income taxes than they should due to lack of a good tax reduction plan. Every business looks for ways to reduce expenses without cutting corners, reducing quality, or losing customers. But few look to the one area almost guaranteed to save you money: income taxes. Last year, America's small businesses overpaid their income taxes by more than 2 billion dollars, according to a CPA study reported in Business 2000 magazine. The overpayments were made because these businesses failed to take the tax deductions they were legally entitled to. Many of these businesses are still unaware of their overpaid taxes, making them susceptible to the same error in the future.

As the IRS does not alert individuals or businesses to tax deductions left unclaimed, it's up to you to protect your financial best interest. This is where my special report comes in. Every strategy explained here will reduce your taxes, honestly, legitimately, and with the full approval of the IRS.

Strategy #1: HSA Plan

One of the most under-utilized tax strategies by businesses is the Health Savings Account (HSA). This account offers a variety of benefits, including:

- **Tax Savings.** HSA's are pretax accounts, and contributions to them are deductible from your gross pay amount, potentially putting you into a lower tax bracket.
- **Tax-free Spending.** Money in an HSA account can be spent for tax-free qualifying health care expenses—a rule that applies for your entire life. Just as with a Roth IRA, withdrawals after retirement are not taxed.
- **Insurance Savings.** The HSA qualifying health insurance policy has a lower premium, allowing you to save money on overall healthcare costs. Moreover, the ability to pay cash for health care costs allows you to negotiate for more affordable services and motivates customers to be healthier. 1
- **Retirement Support.** An HSA can help pay for your retirement. After you turn 65, you have the option to withdraw money for non-health care expenses, and then pay federal income taxes on it. As a HSA holder, you pay ordinary income taxes on nonmedical-related withdrawals, yet with none of the mandatory disbursements required by traditional IRAs.
- **Investment Opportunity.** HSA's allow you to invest money in much the same way you might invest an IRA, as in real estate or a similar venture. It's advisable, though, to stick more with liquid investments if you have a health condition or are at risk of

developing one since you want the money available in case of a medical emergency.

The benefits of HSA's are many, as listed above. These accounts survived the recent federal health-care reform changes—the biggest overhaul of the healthcare system since the 1960's—so it seems a safe bet that HSA's will be around, and available to save you money, for years to come.

These plans are still recognized under ObamaCare as a tax-favored savings account combined with a qualifying high-deductible health insurance plan. It allows taxpayers to get a tax deduction for their healthcare expenses on the front page of their tax returns, enables the unused portions to grow tax free, offers tax-free distributions for healthcare expenses, and, if not used for healthcare, it can be used like a typical IRA after the age of 59 and ½.

It should be noted that in order to reap the tax savings benefit of an HSA plan, the deadline to have one in place is December 1. For example, to receive a deduction during 2013, you have to have a high-deductible health insurance policy ("HDHP") in place by December 1, 2013. You can always fund the HSA up until April 15, 2014, but you must have the insurance policy in place by the December deadline!

Strategy #2: Home Office Write-off

The rules allowing a taxpayer to claim the home office deduction were loosened as of January 1, 1999. No longer does the home office need to be the "principal place of business" for the taxpayer, the qualification can now be satisfied if the taxpayer uses the home office for "administration or management activities" and there is no other fixed location in which the taxpayer performs such activities for his or her business. In other words, the home office still must be used exclusively for business purposes to qualify. This allows more taxpayers, including business owners who conduct business outside of their office but use their home to perform administrative tasks, to qualify for the home office deduction.

Strategy #3: College Education Write-off

For taxpayers challenged with the high cost of providing their children with a college education, this tax strategy is a valuable one to consider. Many business owners don't realize that paying their children under age 18, as well as adult children or grandchildren, is an excellent strategy to minimize their tax liability, in addition to a host of other ancillary benefits.

When children are paid for services they perform for a family business, this generates an expense—i.e. a tax deduction for the parent who is in a much higher tax bracket. The child is in a lower income tax bracket, and so ends up paying little to no tax.

The IRS allows any sole proprietorship or partnership (LLC) that is wholly owned by a child's parents to pay wages to children under age 18 without having to withhold the payroll taxes. For S- and C-Corporations, it is recommended that children be paid out of a family management company that is paid a management fee from the Corporation or out of a Sole-Proprietorship or LLC with independent income and operations. This is because S- and C-Corporations do not receive the benefit of avoiding FICA when payment is made to children; corporate payment to children requires payroll taxes to be withheld. Children over the age of

18 or grandchildren can be treated as sub-contractors or employees, with the employee status requiring FICA withholding and other typical payroll fees. Additionally, the "Kiddie Tax" only applies to unearned or 'portfolio' income (IRC Section. 1(g)(2) (A) and IRC Reg Section 1.1(i)-1T, Q&A 3), disallowing children from being taxed on their income at the parents' rates.

It must be noted that this strategy does not advocate for children's participation in dishonest business operations. Hiring children to simply perform family chores does not qualify as a valid deduction and will certainly lead to an audit. (See U.S. v. Renfrow, 104 AFTR 2d 2009-5497, 1/26/2009). They have to be legitimately involved in the business, records should be kept of their time worked, and they should be paid a reasonable wage. If done correctly, this under-utilized strategy can yield two significant tax advantages.

First, when you pay your children—under the age of 18—to work, you do not have to withhold any income taxes or payroll taxes. (IRC Code Sec. 3121(b)(3)(A), IRC Reg Section 31.3401(a)(4)-1(b), and IRS Pub No. 15, (2011), p.10) The reasons for this are that the government and insurance carriers assume that 1) your children will not sue you if they are hurt on the job, and 2) your children are also probably on your health insurance plan and you would pay the bill one way or another.

Second, no one pay taxes on an initial amount of income earned each year– the Standard 3 Deduction! (For 2013, this figure was $6,100.) (Rev Proc 2011-52, Sec. 3.11(1), 2011-45 IRB). You can still claim your children on your tax return as dependents and take the exemption, even the child tax credit, without your children paying taxes on the first $6,100 of their earned income.

Any income your child earns over and above the standard deduction is taxable at your child's rate. Since the 10 percent tax bracket extends to $8,925 for a single filer, your child could earn an additional $8,925 and owe just $892.50 of federal income tax on the money. Because your marginal tax rate is likely much higher, the extra money your child earns may result in family tax savings.

These accumulated earnings and savings allow you to prioritize your children's futures as you creatively, and legally, prepare for expenses associated with a college education and their other future opportunities. Not only can business owners save thousands of dollars in taxes, but this business setup can draw a family together in ways never fathomed by practicing business owners.

Strategy #4: Roth IRA Eligibility for Kids

This is an incredible, inventive tax saving not often utilized by practitioners that capitalizes on Strategy #3 while taking it a step further. By hiring your children, paying them, and putting the proceeds in a Roth IRA, you are supporting their present and future wellbeing. After all, all earnings in a Roth IRA are tax-free!

Consider this: The U.S. Tax Court has validated a parent hiring his 7-year-old son to work for his business and allowed the deduction for reasonable wages paid. So if your child takes the yearly $5,000, from age 7 to 18, and invests it under the Roth IRA umbrella at 8 percent per year, compounded monthly, that child will have accumulated about $67,000 by age 18.

If you leave all the money untouched, but contribute nothing after your child hits 18, by the time the child is 60, he or she will have accumulated more then $1.9 million that can be withdrawn tax-free.

Strategy #5: Business Retirement Plans

Beyond being a great approach to attract and retain employees, offering a retirement plan is a great way for business owners to shelter income from taxes while saving for retirement. Various studies indicate that only 36 percent of business owners have an IRA, with only one-third of those contributing to it, and less than 20 percent participate in 401(k) plans. This means that business owners do not save enough for their own retirement.

In considering the different needs of different businesses, the tax code offers several types of small business retirement plans. Among the options are:

- **Simplified Employee Pension Plan (SEP).** Under this plan, the employer establishes an IRA for each employee and contributes up to 25 percent of an employee's compensation each year. There is no employee contribution. It's simple, and it's popular with small family-owned businesses.
- **Savings Incentive Match Plan for Employees (SIMPLE).** Companies with fewer than 100 employees can set up a SIMPLE IRA plan. Each employee opens an IRA account, and both employer and employee contribute money to it. There is minimal paperwork and no separate administration fees. It's an efficient way to provide a retirement plan to a large group of people, that is, large by small-business standards.

- **Traditional 401(k) Plan.** This retirement plan allows employees to set aside a portion of their salary for retirement on a pre-tax basis. Designated Roth contributions are also an available option to provide employees the ability to contribute a portion of their salary on an after-tax basis. Companies offering a 401(k) need to file paperwork each year to ensure their plan complies with IRS regulations. But still, a traditional 401(k) Plan is a good option for businesses that plan to grow and want flexibility in how much money the company contributes on behalf of eligible employees.
- **Individual 401(k) Plan.** A 401(k) plan for a company that only has an owner and his/ her spouse, if applicable, with no common law employees. An individual 401(k) plan may allow the owner to set aside more income than other types of retirement plans.
- **Defined Benefit Plan.** Defined Benefit (DB) plans offer business owners the opportunity to save significantly more than they could if using a SEP, SIMPLE or 401k. With a DB plan, the contributions are based on how much income they want at retirement. The DB plan is a great savings tool for a sole proprietor or a business owner with a small number of "rank and file" employees.

Finding the right plan is a critical piece of the retirement savings puzzle. Company-sponsored retirement plans offer the benefits of tax-deferred growth, tax-deductible contributions and high contribution limits. The decision about which plan to choose should be made within the context of your overall goals and the size and profitability of your business.

Strategy #6: Vehicle Deduction

It is not uncommon for business owners to have dedicated vehicles for use by their companies. In such instances, there exists a specific tax loophole designed specifically for business autos in excess of 6,000 pounds.

Since the year-end fiscal cliff deal, 50 percent bonus depreciation once again provides taxpayers the opportunity to immediately deduct half the cost of qualifying assets in the year of acquisition, plus the regular, year-one depreciation on the remaining basis.

For example, if you buy a new piece of machinery for your business in 2013 for $20,000, you may immediately expense $10,000 of the cost and deduct the standard first-year depreciation as determined under the MACRS tables for five-year assets, or $2,000, for a total depreciation deduction of $12,000.

On top of these deductions, business owners may deduct bonus depreciation free from limitation for business autos in excess of 6,000 pounds—which are not subject to the luxury auto limitations and include such popular models as the Chevy Suburban. This strategy offers a simple response to costs associated with an everyday asset that may be applicable to your professional practice.

Strategy #7: Roth Conversions

This strategy highlights how Roth IRAs can be an effective means to business owners achieving their individual retirement goals. Since 2010, all restrictions on converting to a Roth IRA have been removed, regardless of the level of income. For individuals who have been saving for retirement in a traditional IRA, they can now convert some or all of the traditional IRA funds into a Roth IRA.

Converting to a Roth IRA means changing the tax treatment in which your retirement savings are placed, from a tax deferral available with a Traditional IRA to a Roth account with post-tax contributions.

With Roth IRAs, you essentially agree to pay any tax now in exchange for tax-free treatment when the funds are withdrawn later. As Roth IRAs have the potential to grow tax-free, this may help you save more over time. Plus, withdrawals are not mandatory during the lifetime of the original owner, allowing Roth IRA assets to pass to your heirs tax-free.

"The only difference between death and taxes is that death doesn't get worse every time Congress meets." - Will Rogers

"The tax code is a monstrosity and there's only one thing to do with it. Scrap it, kill it, drive a stake through its heart, bury it and hope it never rises again to terrorize the American people." - Steve Forbes

Part II: Profit Maximization

I recently met with two business owners who opened their companies within months of each other. One reported $4.1 million in revenue as well as a high net profit while the other was struggling to keep revenues at $500,000 and trying to manage several cash and employee problems. Reflecting on the disparity of these two businesses, I found myself asking the following question:

How can two businesses operating in the same marketing arena and offering similar services have such extraordinarily different results, with one experiencing continuous growth and prosperity while the other struggles to stay afloat?

Such questions as this one, and the desire to find resolution, are what drive me as a business professional. In my nearly 20-year career, I have cultivated myself as a true business disciple—reading every book imaginable on the subject of business, seeking input from successful entrepreneurs and business experts, attending seminars across the country, and hiring the best businesspeople to advise me. My knowledge and experience has been truly transformational for my clients and can be for you too. In this section of the report, I aim to broaden your awareness regarding certain financial practices that will ensure your business's well-being and longevity.

Strategy #8: Pricing and Fees

Most business owners do not optimally structure their pricing to best benefit their company. The most common mistake is undercharging for services, especially in the context of adjusting rates to match the growth and evolving expenses of a business.

As an example, consider a business owner who has been in practice for 10+ years but who has never raised fees for services—which were most likely originally priced competitively low to attract customers and build the business. With a simple 15 percent increase across the board in service prices—well-deserved for a business that emphasizes quality and value in its customer care—that business owner is adding tens of thousands of dollars in revenue each year. Every dollar generated after fixed expenses are covered contributes mightily toward a business's net profit.

Though it is important to be competitive at the outset of a business, it is even more critical not to allow the lure of low prices outweigh the ability to provide quality and sustain a company in the long term. The right pricing can have a big impact on the profitability of a small business. It's necessary to strike a balance. Overpricing can certainly deter customers, but under pricing cuts into profits, which is a huge disservice to a business and the professionals it supports.

Instead, attract new customers based on such aspects as care quality, level of service, and turn-around time.

Strategy #9: Accounting Firm Compatibility

A compatible accounting firm is integral to a business's success. The truth is that accountants, CPAs, and tax preparers are **not** all the same. Most accountants spend the majority of their time with their clients' monthly bookkeeping work, tax forms filing, and mundane compliance work—all of which takes time away from paying attention to the unique financial and tax needs of a business. Accountants are often overworked, understaffed, and generally overwhelmed during tax season as they fight against the clock each year to complete all their clients' returns. It can be difficult to tell whether they are doing their best work or simply working. As you consider who you want to partner with for the strength and success of your business, consider the following things:

- When you talk with your accountant, are you getting his or her **full attention**?
- Does your tax professional **really understand your business**?
- Is your accountant giving you advice that **increases profits, reduces taxes, and protects your assets**?
- Does your accountant ensure there are **no red flags** for the IRS to audit your business?
- Does your accountant **specialize** in areas relevant to your business?

If you answered "NO" to any of these questions, then it may be time to reconsider in whose hands you are entrusting your business. As you strive to be the best professional and best business owner you can be, help yourself by partnering with a compatible accounting firm—one that understands your work and can guide you in reducing your taxes, maximizing your profits, and protecting your assets.

Strategy #10: Effective Accounting System

Every business needs an effective accounting system. Many owners overlook the logical method of tracking their revenues and expenses by "profit centers." A financial reporting system should be set up such that it has the ability to generate reports that provide a breakdown of revenues and expenses by type of service provided or type of product sold— i.e. by each profit center.

Once an effective accounting system is established, it serves as the foundation of your company, tracking the financial health of a business so it can grow and change as it needs to. To be effective, there are four basic requirements an accounting system must meet:

- Be **simple to use and easy to understand**. The information will be kept current if the system is "user-friendly."
- **Maintain relevant and accurate records**. The system should be specific to your business in order to minimize time-recording information; should record only what is necessary; and should be free of errors.
- **Ensure that records are kept current**. The information will only be effective if records are done in a timely fashion.
- **Keep records that exhibit consistent standards and principles**. The same standards and principles should be followed throughout the system, and at all times.

As you consider implementing an accounting system, be sure it allows you to perform all these functions to best support your business. A strong financial management system, such as QuickBooks, is the cornerstone of any prosperous company. Setting up QuickBooks correctly from the start will save time and allow you to get more out of the software. Desert Rose Tax & Accounting has successfully set up this software in many businesses across Arizona, and the yields and benefits have been incredible.

Strategy #11: Financial Responsibility

This strategy is a core part of a business owner's individual success and success in an accounting partnership. In sharing financial responsibility, business owners are both freed up to focus on their professional duties while also remaining integral in core operational considerations.

Even if you hire someone to handle your accounting and bookkeeping there are still some things you, as the business owner, should not totally surrender responsibility for. The following are guidelines for you to use on a regular basis:

- **Compare actual results to budget**. Each and every, month compare your income and expenses to the budget. It is a great way to learn what is and what is not working with 11 your company. The goal is not to have an accurate budget, but for you to have a thorough working knowledge of what is happening and be prepared for anything unexpected.
- **Look at canceled checks**. Occasionally (1-2 times a year) conduct a thorough review of your bank statements, making sure to flip through the canceled checks. Ensure that all signatures are yours and that you recognize the vendors. Be sure to scan the endorsements on the back.
- **Review payroll register and hand out the paychecks**. In some industries, "padding" the payroll is a common problem. Regular review of the payroll register will prevent this from occurring and handing out paychecks will keep you personally engaged with the payroll process.
- **Review your Accounts Receivable and aging**. Check for "slow paying" customers and make sure customer payments are being correctly applied. And, on a more personal level that will also serve to protect you financially:

- **Delegate duties**. Have a clear idea of how you want duties delegated across your staff so that there is a clear understanding of each person's role in the business, with your expectations the forefront of all operations.
- **Know your employees**. Surround yourself with capable individuals who you trust to ensure transparency and smooth operations. Be aware of each staff member's use of and interaction with finances and resources so that there is a culture of accountability.

Strategy #12: Gross vs. Net

Very few people recognize the difference between **gross** and **net** when it comes to finances. In business, where gross refers to the total income, net refers to income after all expenses, overheads, taxes, and interest payments are deducted. The difference in value between these two amounts can be significant.

As the head of your business, it is important for you to know the difference between the two; to see how gross and net express themselves in the context of your company; and to have someone who emphasizes profit and net worth over gross figures, and who helps you to track and measure both constantly.

Very few professionals spend enough time analyzing, and re-analyzing, what parts of their 12 business—what services, what customers, what facilities—are the most net profitable. Business owners often allow low-profit considerations to consume the same resources as high profit once, paying exorbitant amounts of money for unnecessarily large offices, an excessive number of staff, and other features used to impress people without profitable purpose.

For the health of your business, it is incumbent upon you—and your accounting team—to consider your expenses and ask questions such as, "How does this contribute to net?" and "How much does this contribute to net?" Because without net viability, all other perceived benefits are unsubstantial.

Strategy #13: Tracking Critical Numbers

Tracking the CRITICAL numbers and indicators in your company is one of the best, most important things you can do as a business owner. What is not measured cannot be improved, but in keeping a financial dashboard that tracks core figures, you can carve a niche for your business that fosters a competitive advantage.

There are two sets of numbers that every business owner should keep and look at on a very regular basis: **lagging numbers** and **leading numbers**. Lagging numbers, or indicators, are historical in nature and do not give much visibility to the business. Lagging numbers include gross revenues by day, week, month, quarter and year, gross margin; and net profit.

While these are important indicators and all businesses should closely monitor them because they reveal a company's overall trajectory and level of success, leading numbers inform a company's performance. Examples of leading numbers include:

- Lifetime value, or the total profit of an average customer over the lifetime of his or her patronage (See Strategy #15)
- Money spent by customers per year
- Number of new leads and how they were derived
- Percentage of leads that converted to customers
- Marketing cost to attain leads 13

- Marketing cost per customer
- Projected revenues
- Projected expenses

Leading numbers give more insight into the business as a means of making good, day-to-day decisions. In other words, these are indicators of what is happening, magnified so you can clearly see and understand.

Strategy #14: Cash vs. Profit

In approaching business, people generally think in profits instead of cash. When imagining a new start-up company, a business owner thinks of the cost to promote the products and services, the fee that could be charged, and what the profits per unit might be. They are trained to think of a company as sales minus costs and expenses—that is, profit. Unfortunately, profits are not spent in business—cash is.

Profitable companies go broke every day because money is tied up in assets and expenses can't be paid for. Working capital is critical to the health of your business. It is critical that you see the cash implications of your company as clearly as possible, which is one of the best reasons for proper cash planning. You must **manage cash**, as well as profits.

Strategy #15: Customer's Lifetime Value

The lifetime value of a customer is one of the most valuable things a business owner can know. It is simply the total profit of an average customer over the lifetime of his or her patronage, including all back-end sales less all advertising, marketing, and incremental product or service fulfillment expenses.

For example, each new customer brings you an average profit of $100 on the first visit. He or she follows your prescribed program and revisits ten more times a year, with an average profit of $75 on each visit. Now, with the average patronage lasting two years, every new customer is worth $1,600: {$100 + (10 x $75) + (10 x $75)} = $1,600. This calculation is critical to your business. By knowing what the value of an average customer is, you can then determine two things:

- How much you can afford to spend to acquire a new customer.
- How much you can afford to spend to keep an existing customer from leaving you for your competitor.

There are two important lessons here and understanding them will make a HUGE difference in your business.

The first lesson is that the amount you can theoretically afford to spend to bring in a new customer is the same as the approximate value of a customer. If the lifetime value of a customer is $1,600, you can afford to spend up to $1,600 to bring in a new customer and still break even, depending on the profitability of your company. This is an important number to know as you make important business decisions on what media to advertise in, how to compensate your staff (particularly those who interface with customers most often), and what fees to charge for your services.

The second lesson is that the key to keeping customers is to develop a long-term relationship with them. A customer on your database is not merely a name but a real person with changing and evolving needs and wants, and they are being constantly bombarded with multiple other options. Always consider the lifetime value of your customers and do whatever it takes to retain their loyalty. Find ways to incorporate that value in your office as a constant reminder to you and your staff of how important each and every customer is to your business.

Strategy #16: The Trap of ONE

Becoming too reliant on one employee, one vendor, one customer, or one marketing avenue is a common pitfall of businesses. Consider the lesser risk of having 100 clients paying $1,000 each than one client paying $100,000. The same rule applies to employees, vendors, and the number of ways to attract new customers. In business, diversity is key to combating stagnancy.

Following is an example as a cautionary tale: A business owner built a substantial book of customers by using a particular mailing piece to attract new customers who had recently moved into the area. Over time, other local business owners caught on to this approach and copied the marketing piece. Literally overnight, the response from the business owner's mailing campaign—upon which he had relied heavily for business—dropped dramatically. The mistake he had made was not developing other methods to obtain leads, thus making him susceptible to professional attrition and causing his business to decline substantially.

In the long run, it's better to know 20 different ways to bring a new client into your company than to put weight your efforts too heavily in one way. It is actually **easier and more realistic** to devise 20 little ways to get one new customer at a time as compared to achieving an immediate, mass response with one marketing ad.

Strategy #17: Customer Referrals

Customer referrals are a non-stop way of creating steady streams of prospects and clients. Referral customers are the most profitable, cost-efficient, loyal, and continuous source of new business you will ever access. They also are the most reliable, often paying the most money, negotiating fees the least, following your prescribed programs, and referring even more of the best people to you.

In knowing the importance of customer referrals, the **E.A.R.** formula is a powerful concept to help you encourage referrals on behalf of your own business. E.A.R. stands for **Earn, Ask, and Reward**. Every business should exhibit at least one aspect of the E.A.R. formula as a natural extension of its normal approach to customer care.

If you are good at what you do, you will naturally earn more business because your customers will talk positively about you. By taking care of your customers, you **earn the right to ask**. If confident in the service and care you provide, you should have no problem **asking for referrals**. And if you have earned your customers' approval and been able to ask for referrals, you should **reward your customers** for their help. You will be surprised at the loyalty your customers show when you offer them recognition in response for their patronage!

Strategy #18: Meaningful Touches

How many times should a business be in touch with its customers in the course of a year, not including face-to-face visits for service? Answers vary but rarely if ever do they exceed eight or nine times per year. An ideal number is 24 times per year, based on the following breakdown:

Monthly newsletter	12
Birthday card or gift	1
Anniversary of business relationship	1
Thanksgiving card	1
Thank-you postcard	2
Special offers and referral offers	5
Personal phone calls	2

Contact with your customer should be frequent, constant, unrelenting communication using every media available—direct mail, fax, email, phone calls, and more. Keep your customers engaged and wondering, "What will I be sent next?!" If you desire to go the extra mile, have an annual event in appreciation for your customers. The results, such as raving fans and new clients thorough referrals, can be extremely positive for your business.

Strategy #19: Customer-centric Services

An important way for a company to increase its number of customers is to keep existing customers from seeking other options. By emphasizing quality, paying close attention to what customers say, and responding to customer needs, companies can keep customers from slipping away to competition or less effective services.

The Marketing Science Institute of Cambridge, Massachusetts asked customers from a wide range of businesses what factors they considered most important in assuring their satisfaction. Responses included the following:

- **Reliability**. This topped the list of what customers expect. A major source of customer dissatisfaction is the "unkept promise."
- **Responsiveness**. Customers desire service to be helpful and provide prompt.
- **Assurance**. Employees should be knowledgeable and courteous and should convey confidence in the service they provide.
- **Empathy**. Customers want individualized attention and people who will listen to them.
- **Tangibles**. Physical facilities and equipment should be attractive and clean. Employees should be well dressed and well groomed.

Strategy #20: Effective Communication

According to a recent Gallup Survey, the six most common complaints clients have about businesses are:

- **Over-promising and under-delivering**. Most companies are guilty of this one but few companies understand its danger.
- **Failing to stay in touch**. Clients appreciate it when businesses keep in contact, viewing communication as a sign that their patronage is appreciated and that they, as individuals, are valued.
- **Using too much industry jargon**. It is easy to assume that clients know as much about an industry as business owners do. The truth is, they don't. The difference is that clients do generally know what their own wants and needs are. This demands businesses speak and write so that information is easy for clients to understand.
- **Failing to listen to customers' concerns/ideas**. The best expression to recall is: we have two ears, one mouth. When it

comes to their clients, business owners should listen twice as much as they talk.
- **Explaining rather then telling**. Clients and patrons do not like to be sold. They want to be educated so they can then decide what is best for them. Telling is selling. Explaining is educating.
- **Communicating without courtesy**. Businesses should always remember to be polite in all communication, written and spoken. Courtesy is key to keeping clients happy and should never be underestimated in any interaction.

Food for thought:

In his book Keeping Customers for Life, Richard F. Gerson breaks down the reasons why companies lose customers, with the vast majority—**68 percent**—leaving on account of displeasure with the treatment they received. That's a significant number warranting a lot of attention.

In your approach to customer care, make sure customers' concerns are also your concerns. Think about the various services you employ and interactions you have on a regular basis: an attendant at a store, a clerk in the grocery store checkout line, the crew on a flight, and the staff in a hotel. Which interactions are the most rewarding or meaningful for you—ones where you feel ignored or tended to? The same considerations should factor into your customers' interactions with your business. If you are losing customers, find out why and find out quickly. Pay attention to how you provide for them. Let them know you care.

Strategy #21: Pay Yourself First

A business owner must never settle for what is left over. As owner of a company, you are 18 at the center of its success. Though the urge may exist to take care of other costs and expenses first, it is critical that you prioritize your needs and role within the business. Once you are properly paid, the profit can be dedicated to other expenditures. If the leftovers are not enough to support all of your expenses, reduce staff and cut costs.

You must not con yourself into nothing now for more later. Take a pre-determined percentage of every dollar off the very, very top and move it away from your business. Do not spend it, but place it in illiquid, untouchable, sound investments. A business is a cash-generating asset to take wealth out of, not just have wealth locked up in. If you can't take at least 1 percent off the top now, there will be nothing for later.

Strategy #22: Systemize to Reduce Stress

One of the most important things a business owner can do is systemize operations for the long term, considering how things might function in the owner's absence. Ensuring that your business operates like a finely tuned machine will open it to untold achievement. Having systems in place that support long-term plans and account for a variety of circumstances is the ultimate way to run a business.

What is a system? A system is something that describes and spells out how things are done at your business, often taking the shape of a "policies and procedures" manual. The benefits of documenting a system include being able to deliver service in a predictable and consistent way; allowing you, as the owner, to have a life; and making it easier to sell the company if or when the time comes. Ultimately, your company is a system of systems. Most businesses can be broken down into the following six distinct areas:

- **Leadership.** Articulating a vision or mission statement, and living it.

- **Marketing**. Defining who your customers are within analytical/statistical areas: income, age, ethnicity, geographical locations, etc.
- **Management**. Producing the service; recruiting and training staff; taking care of the facilities.
- **Money**. Keeping track of key financial reports and critical financial numbers.
- **Lead Generation**. Attracting customers; employing various advertising methods to establish leads.
- **Client Fulfillment**. Delivering what is promised, in the form of services and products, consistently and predictably.

Using this structure will allow you to begin delegating yourself out of certain responsibilities; open you up to more individual freedom. The bottom line is that you did not open your business so it would control your life! You want your business to serve you, not the other way around.

"Wealth is well known to be a great comforter." - Plato

"Wealth, like happiness, is never attained when sought after directly. It comes as a by-product of providing a useful service." - Henry Ford

Part III: Asset Protection

Lawsuits and audits present tremendous susceptibilities when it comes to the protection of assets, and of the individuals who hold those assets. For business owners, the stakes are high—with financial, physical, personnel, and other responsibilities falling on them as leaders and protectors of their companies. Not only are there tangibles and monetary investments to consider, but owners' personal lives are often deeply entrenched in their work.

Every year millions of people are sued. It is estimated that a new lawsuit is filed every 30 seconds in the U.S., and there are over 100 million lawsuits currently in the court system. With the number of lawsuits and the size of judgments on the rise, it is vital to have your professional and personal assets structured for lawsuit protection.

Although the overall number of audits the IRS is performing declined in recent years (due to an overall increase in the number of tax returns filed each year), audits of incomes over $200,000 and over $1 million increased in fiscal year 2012, and corporate tax returns remain at high levels by historic standards. As a business owner, your company's economic well-being—and your own! —is dependent upon best processes in financial management and tax preparation. In order to avoid an audit, or in the event one occurs, you want to be sure that all financial aspects of your business are legally and ethically prepared for a potential IRS inquisition.

In this section of the report, I will share with you how to protect 100 percent of your assets from lawsuits and audits. These strategies will also prevent lawsuits by showing you how to make yourself unattractive to a plaintiff attorney such that they will never pursue a lawsuit against you, as well as some basic tips on guarding yourself against audit scrutiny. Once your assets are properly structured, you will have financial peace of mind that comes from knowing that you are protected from losing what you have worked a lifetime to create.

Strategy #23: Protective Legal Structure

A 2001 survey found that more than 50 percent of business owners were practicing without the benefit of legal structures, leaving them vulnerable to a host of non-medical liabilities. Beyond lawsuits related to certain professions, businesses set up as sole proprietorships and general partnerships leave business owners personally liable for a judgment in lawsuits staked on something as simple as a trip and fall or issues like wrongful termination, sexual harassment, and discrimination. If 50 percent of U.S. companies are sole proprietorships, these business owners are personally exposed to unlimited legal liability in their business operations

Strategy #24: Diversified Protection

What the 50 percent of business owners operating with the benefit of legal structures may not realize is that operating under just one all-inclusive legal identity—such as a professional corporation (PC), professional association (PA), C- or S-corporation, or a limited liability company—can be just as risky.

The new rule of lawsuit protection is simple: Keep your business assets separate from your business operations. This means that cash-rich assets, such as buildings and land, should be kept in separate legal entities, such as limited partnerships, to avoid one lawsuit from draining a corporation entirely. Professional corporations should instead own as few assets as possible so they do not become a target of litigation.

There is no right or wrong way to diversify and there are many variables to consider for a company: How many business owners are part of the company? Are the building and land owned or leased? What is the value of the professional equipment? Following are some general principles:

First, divide **your business assets from your business operations**. Review carefully the nature of your company and professional activities to determine whether you can logically divide the company or professional activity into two or more separate entities.

Second, keep your **personal life separate from your professional life.** If private and professional assets are mixed, both are made vulnerable in lawsuits.

Third, **structure yourself to withstand litigation before a lawsuit occurs**. Any steps to rearrange your assets after a potential lawsuit occurs can be ruled fraudulent by the courts. Using asset protection principles before a problem arises, however, is both smart and strategic.

As you restructure your assets, make sure your lawyer is fully versed in the modern asset protection principles specific to your company. Statistically, less than one-tenth of one percent of all lawyers even claim to specialize in this area. Asset protection is too important to leave to chance. Few professionals have as much to gain from asset protection as private business owners today, operating with a variety of liabilities. Engage the vulnerabilities of your business with eyes wide open, realizing that you can use the legal system to protect yourself instead of being abused by it.

Strategy #25: Audit Protection

Audits are on the rise and the goal is to make sure that business owners can rightfully defend themselves and their businesses should an audit take place. If the right measures aren't taken, an audit can wipe out an entire company. Here are some basic principles to adhere to:

- **Good record keeping.** Being able to substantiate all the deductions you take on your tax return with invoices and other records will always help your cause. Additionally, track your expenses in such a way that you can prove an expense was ordinary and necessary.
- **Accurate financial statements.** Financial statements provide a formal record of your business and its financial activities, offering valuable information about your company's strengths, weaknesses, and overall financial position. In the event of an audit, all of your company's financial statements will likely be requested, in which case your commitment to accuracy will protect against the types of misuse or misappropriation of funds that commonly incur legal action.
- **No red flags.** Large amounts of money in certain expense categories, such as meals, entertainment, travel, office expenses, etc., may trigger an audit. Be sure that your finances

are appropriately attributed and documented as such, to avoid red flags upon annual review of your tax returns.

"Avoid lawsuits beyond all things; they pervert your conscience, impair your health, and dissipate your property." - Jean de la Bruyere

"Frivolous lawsuits are booming in this country. The U.S. has more costs of litigations per person than any other industrialized nation in the world, and it is crippling our economy." - Jack Kingston

Next Steps

Financial Freedom is Only One Step Away

I hope you have found the strategies I shared in this report helpful. Each one is meant to provide you with information, suggestions, and tips that you can rely on, implement, and use as a barometer for success and strength in your business. The strategies contained within this report reflect knowledge and experience gained through my business career that is further tailored by my extensive work with business owners and their companies. As a next step, I invite you to register for my free, no-obligation strategy session:

Tax Reduction, Profit Maximization, and Asset Protection

When professional business owners like you come to me, I re-examine their past three years of tax returns and, **80 percent** of the time, I find multiple mistakes, missed deductions, overpayments and red flags. These errors are a result of the work of accountants who do not intimately and completely understand YOUR Company.

At the end of the day, these errors add up to money that should be in your pocket but isn't. Money you could put away for your children's education ... money you could spend on trips with your family ... money you could put away for your financial nest egg for early retirement ... money you could use for a new house, a new car, hobbies that you enjoy ... **money that gives you the financial security and lifestyle you deserve.**

My free strategy session aims to help you slash your taxes, keep more of your hard-earned money, and feel confident that your assets are fully protected. If you find yourself questioning whether you are **getting the attention you deserve** from your accountant; whether your tax professional **truly understands your business** and all its intricacies; or whether you are **receiving advice that actually benefits you**, this strategy session is exactly what you need.

Think of this: You have nothing to lose and SO MUCH to gain from this session.

During your 50-minute, one-on-one appointment with me, I will evaluate your taxes with a keen eye and point out any mistakes that are costing you money or putting you at risk of an audit. As an experienced financial and tax consultant for business owners, I will reveal to you the most common areas I have found where business owners overpay their taxes, miss opportunities to increase their net take-home pay, and are susceptible to unwanted attention from the IRS. I will then personally walk you through the critical steps you must take in order to protect your assets.

If, after your FREE Tax **Reduction, Profit Maximization, and Asset**

Protection strategy session, you decide to engage my help on an ongoing basis, you will receive a **free, comprehensive re-examination of three years of tax returns with a full satisfaction guarantee**. Reserve your spot for our session by completing the page titled "Free Strategy Session

I look forward to meeting you soon.

Warm Regards,

Joseph D Rose, CPA, CTC

Your Roadmap to Success

As you prepare for your free strategy session, use the following roadmap of the strategies contained within this report to predetermine areas where you may want or need to focus our conversation.

o Strategy #1: HSA Plan

o Strategy #2: Home Office Write-off

o Strategy #3: College Education Write-off

o Strategy #4: Roth IRA Eligibility for Kids

o Strategy #5: Business Retirement Plans

o Strategy #6: Vehicle Deduction

o Strategy #7: Roth Conversions

o Strategy #8: Pricing and Fees

o Strategy #9: Accounting Firm Compatibility

o Strategy #10: Effective Accounting System

o Strategy #11: Financial Responsibility

o Strategy #12: Gross vs. Net

o Strategy #13: Tracking Critical Numbers

- Strategy #14: Cash vs. Profits
- Strategy #15: Customer's Lifetime Value
- Strategy #16: The Trap of ONE
- Strategy #17: Customer Referrals
- Strategy #18: Meaningful Touches
- Strategy #19: Customer-centric Services
- Strategy #20: Effective Communication
- Strategy #21: Pay Yourself First
- Strategy #22: Systemize to Reduce Stress
- Strategy #23: Protective Legal Structure
- Strategy #24: Diversified Protection
- Strategy #25: Audit Protection

Free Strategy Session for Tax Reduction, Profit Maximization & Asset Protection

oYes, Joseph, please reserve my spot... for a free, 50-minute, one-on-one Tax-Reduction, Profit Maximization, and Asset Protection strategy session. Act fast, as only five business owners have this opportunity each month due to space and time constraints. The strategy session covers such topics as:

• How to predictably slash your tax bill by 20-30 percent each year;

• How current government tax plans is affecting business how to keep more of your hard-earned money;

• Simple ways to save thousands by legally reducing your tax;

• How to avoid spending extra years working just to pay taxes;

• Secrets to mitigating the devastating effects of taxation on your family's income; and

• Effective structuring for asset protection and tax minimization.

Where individualized strategy sessions typically require payment, this is a very special offer at an incredible value.

Please complete the following information:

Name:
_____

Business name:
_____

Address:
_____

Phone _____ Fax _____ Email _____

Best way to reach you: _____

Best day/s to meet (circle below)

Monday   Tuesday   Wednesday   Thursday   Friday

Morning   Afternoon

Submit via:

- Fax to (520) 747-4968

- Phone to (520) 747-4964

www. DesertRoseTax.com

ABOUT THE AUTHOR

Joseph D Rose, CPA, CTC

Joseph is the president and founder of Desert Rose Tax & Accounting, PC. He is a Certified Tax Coach helping individuals and businesses in the Tucson and surrounding area reduce their tax burden with proactive strategies for over twenty years.

Joseph is a graduate of the University of Arizona with a Bachelor of Science in Business Administration majoring in Accounting. He is licensed in Arizona as a Certified Public Accountant and is a member in good standing with both the American Institute of Certified Public Accountants & the Arizona Society of Certified Public Accountants.

Joseph began his professional career as a controller of Envirocycle Management Service Technologies, a Tucson Arizona based engineering firm. He simultaneously implemented a strategic plan and began developing a tax business focused on helping small businesses navigate the complex world of income tax and reduce their tax burden.

Using his business experience and education, Joseph is in a perfect position to help small businesses improve operations by making the most of their resources. He also helps analyze strategies and opportunities which exist to help business owners maximize their tax savings.

Joseph is passionate about proactive tax planning being the key to reducing taxes. He has spent hundreds of hours of continuing education to ensure he provides the best solutions for his clients. Over the years Joseph has helped hundreds of business owners save hundreds of thousands in tax savings. He has given seminars on proactive tax planning as well as written a number of articles on the topic.

In addition to educating clients, Joseph generously supports several local charities with his time, knowledge and resources. He is very involved in his church having served on several committees and task forces. Joseph is married with four children and three grandchildren.

He can be reached at (520) 747-4964 or by email at info@desertrosetax.com. You may also visit his website at www.desertrosetax.com.

www.ingramcontent.com/pod-product-compliance
Lightning Source LLC
Chambersburg PA
CBHW070415190526
45169CB00003B/1266